by Catherine Baker

illustrated by Cinta Villalobos

Dad had a big wooden shed.

"It looks a bit drab," said Dad.

"Let me help!" said Fern.
"I can put a big picture on it."

"Yes!" said Dad.
"A picture will look good there."

Fern was not sure what picture to pick.

Perhaps put some herbs on it!
That will not look good.

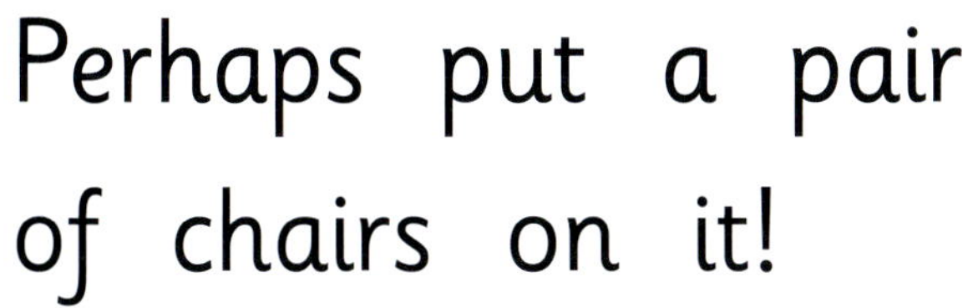
Perhaps put a pair of chairs on it!
That is too hard!

Perhaps put some sheep on it!
That is a bit dull.

At last, Fern had a plan!

“What will the picture be?” said Dad.

"You must wait and see!" said Fern.

Fern and Mum got things from the shed.

The picture went along the shed.
It got longer and longer!

It took them all morning to finish.

Fern was keen to show Dad.

"Come and see my picture!" said Fern.

It was a big dragon!

Encourage students to use the pictures to retell the story.